MATHS FORMULA LIST

THIS BOOK CONTAILS ALMOST ALL THE FORMULAE REQUIRED IN ICSE CLASS 9

SAMARTH AGRAWAL

Class 9 Maths Formulas For Rational Numbers

Any number that can be written in the form of p/q where p and q are integers and q ≠ 0 are rational numbers. Irrational numbers cannot be written in the p/q form.

There is a unique real number which can be represented on a number line.

If r is one such rational number and s is an irrational number, then (r + s), (r − s), (r × s) and (r/s) are irrational.

For positive real numbers, the corresponding identities hold together:

$$ab\text{---}\sqrt{ab} = a\text{---}\sqrt{}\times b\sqrt{}a\times b$$

$$ab\text{---}\sqrt{ab} = a\sqrt{b}\sqrt{ab}$$

$$(a\text{---}\sqrt{}+b\sqrt{})\times(a\text{---}\sqrt{}-b\sqrt{})=a-b(a+b)\times(a-b)=a-b$$

$$(a+b\sqrt{})\times(a-b\sqrt{})=a2-b(a+b)\times(a-b)=a2-b$$

$$(a\text{---}\sqrt{}+b\sqrt{})2=a2+2ab\text{---}\sqrt{}+b(a+b)2=a2+2ab+b$$

If you want to rationalize the denominator of 1/√ (a + b), then we have to multiply it by √(a − b)/√(a − b), where a and b are both the integers.

Suppose a is a real number (greater than 0) and p and q are the rational numbers.

$$ap \times bq = (ab)p+q$$

$$(a^p)^q = a^{pq}$$

$$a^p / a^q = (a)^{p-q}$$

$$a^p / b^p = (ab)^p$$

Class 9 Maths Formulas For Polynomials

A polynomial p(x) denoted for one variable 'x' comprises an algebraic expression in the form:

$$p(x) = a_n x^n + a_{n-1} x^{n-1} + ... + a_2 x^2 + a_1 x + a_0 \; ; \text{ where } a_0, a_1, a_2, ... a_n$$
are constants where $a_n \neq 0$

Any real number; let's say 'a' is considered to be the zero of a polynomial 'p(x)' if p(a) = 0. In this case, a is said to be the root of the equation p(x) = 0.

Every one variable linear polynomial will contain a unique zero, a real number which is a zero of the zero polynomial and non-zero constant polynomial which does not have any zeros.

Remainder Theorem: If p(x) has the degree greater than or equal to 1 and p(x) when divided by the linear polynomial x − a will give the remainder as p(a).

Factor Theorem: x − a will be the factor of the polynomial p(x), whenever p(a) = 0. The vice-versa also holds true every time.

Class 9 Maths Formulas For Coordinate Geometry

Whenever you have to locate an object on a plane, you need two divide the plane into two perpendicular lines, thereby, making it a

Cartesian Plane.

The horizontal line is known as the x-axis and the vertical line is called the y-axis.

The coordinates of a point are in the form of (+, +) in the first quadrant, (−, +) in the second quadrant, (−, −) in the third quadrant and (+, −) in the fourth quadrant; where + and − denotes the positive and the negative real number respectively.

The coordinates of the origin are (0, 0) and thereby it gets up to move in the positive and negative number.

9th Class Formulas For Algebraic Identities

Given below are the algebraic identities which are considered very important maths formulas for Class 9.

$$(a + b)2 = a2 + 2ab + b2$$

$$(a - b)2 = a2 - 2ab + b2$$

$$(a + b) (a - b) = a2 - b2$$

$$(x + a) (x + b) = x2 + (a + b) x + ab$$

$$(x + a) (x - b) = x2 + (a - b) x - ab$$

$$(x - a) (x + b) = x2 + (b - a) x - ab$$

$$(x - a) (x - b) = x2 - (a + b) x + ab$$

$$(a + b)3 = a3 + b3 + 3ab (a + b)$$

$$(a - b)3 = a3 - b3 - 3ab (a - b)$$

$$(x + y + z)2 = x2 + y2 + z2 + 2xy +2yz + 2xz$$

$$(x + y - z)2 = x2 + y2 + z2 + 2xy - 2yz - 2xz$$

$$(x - y + z)2 = x2 + y2 + z2 - 2xy - 2yz + 2xz$$

$$(x - y - z)2 = x2 + y2 + z2 - 2xy + 2yz - 2xz$$

$$x3 + y3 + z3 - 3xyz = (x + y + z) (x2 + y2 + z2 - xy - yz -xz)$$

$$x2 + y2 = 1212 [(x + y)2 + (x - y)2]$$

$$(x + a) (x + b) (x + c) = x3 + (a + b + c)x2 + (ab + bc + ca)x + abc$$

$$x3 + y3 = (x + y) (x2 - xy + y2)$$

$$x3 - y3 = (x - y) (x2 + xy + y2)$$

$$x2 + y2 + z2 - xy - yz - zx = 1212 [(x - y)2 + (y - z)2 + (z - x)2]$$

Class 9 Maths Formulas For Triangles

A triangle is a closed geometrical figure formed by three sides and three angles.

Two figures are congruent if they have the same shape and same size.

If the two triangles ABC and DEF are congruent under the correspondence that A ↔ D, B ↔ E and C ↔ F, then symbolically, these can be expressed as $\triangle$ ABC $\cong$ $\triangle$ DEF.

Right Angled Triangle: Pythagoras Theorem

Suppose Δ ABC is a right-angled triangle with AB as the perpendicular, BC as the base and AC as the hypotenuse; then Pythagoras Theorem will be expressed as:

$$(\text{Hypotenuse})^2 = (\text{Perpendicular})^2 + (\text{Base})^2$$
$$\text{i.e. } (AC)^2 = (AB)^2 + (BC)^2$$

Class 9 Maths Formulas For Areas Of Parallelograms And Triangles

A parallelogram is a type of quadrilateral which contains parallel opposite sides.

$$\text{Area of parallelogram} = \text{Base} \times \text{Height}$$

$$\text{Area of Triangle} = \frac{1}{2} \times \text{Base} \times \text{Height}$$

Class 9 Maths Formulas For Circle

A circle is a closed geometrical figure. All points on the boundary of a circle are equidistance from a fixed point inside the circle (called the centre).

$$\text{Area of a circle (of radius } r) = \pi \times r^2$$

$$\text{The diameter of the circle, } d = 2 \times r$$

$$\text{Circumference of the circle} = 2 \times \pi \times r$$

$$\text{Sector angle of the circle, } \theta = (180 \times l) / (\pi \times r)$$

Area of the sector = $(\theta/2) \times r2$; where θ is the angle between the two radii

Area of the circular ring = $\pi \times (R2 - r2)$; where R – radius of the outer circle and r – radius of the inner circle

Class 9 Maths Heron's Formula

Heron's Formula is used to calculate the area of a triangle whose all three sides are known. Let's suppose the length of three sides are a, b and c.

Step 1 – Calculate the semi-perimeter, s=a+b+c2s=a+b+c2

Step 2 – Area of the triangle =
s(s−a)(s−b)(s−c)––––––––––––––––––√s(s−a)(s−b)(s−c)

Class 9 Maths Formulas For Surface Areas And Volumes

Here, LSA stands for Lateral/Curved Surface Area and TSA stands for Total Surface Area.

Name of the Solid FigureFormulas

CuboidLSA: 2h(l + b)
TSA: 2(lb + bh + hl)
Volume: l × b × h

l = length,
b = breadth,
h = height

CubeLSA: 4a2
TSA: 6a2
Volume: a3

a = sides of a cube

Right Circular CylinderLSA: 2(π × r × h)
TSA: 2πr (r + h)
Volume: π × r2 × h

r = radius,
h = height

Right PyramidLSA: ½ × p × l
TSA: LSA + Area of the base
Volume: ⅓ × Area of the base × h

p = perimeter of the base,
l = slant height, h = height

PrismLSA: p × h
TSA: LSA × 2B
Volume: B × h

p = perimeter of the base,
B = area of base, h = height

Right Circular ConeLSA: πrl
TSA: π × r × (r + l)
Volume: ⅓ × (πr2h)

r = radius,

l = slant height,

h = height

HemisphereLSA: 2 × π × r2

TSA: 3 × π × r2

Volume: ⅔ × (πr3)

r = radius

SphereLSA: 4 × π × r2

TSA: 4 × π × r2

Volume: 4/3 × (πr3)

r = radius

Class 9 Maths Formulas For Statistics

Certain facts or figures which can be collected or transformed into some useful purpose are known as data. These data can be graphically represented to increase readability for people.

Three measures of formulas to interpret the ungrouped data:

CategoryMathematical Formulas

Mean, x̄ x̄ ∑xn∑xn

x = Sum of the values; N = Number of values

Standard Deviation,

σσσ=∑ni=1(xi−x̄)2N−1−−−−−−−−−√σ=∑i=1n(xi−x̄)2N−1

x_i = Terms Given in the Data, $\bar{x}$ = Mean, N = Total number of Terms

Range, RR = Largest data value − Smallest data value

Variance, $\sigma^2\sigma^2\sigma^2 = \sum x_i - x^- N\sigma^2 = \sum x_i - x^- N$

x = Item given in the data, $\bar{x}$ = Mean of the data,
n = Total number of items

Class 9 Maths Formulas For Probability

Probability is the possibility of any event likely to happen. The probability of any event can only be from 0 to 1 with 0 being no chances and 1 being the possibility of that event to happen.

Probability=Number of favourable outcomes / Total Number of outcomes

Contents

Prologue

Class 9 Maths Formulas For Rational Numbers

Any number that can be written in the form of p / q where p and q are integers and q ≠ 0 are rational numbers. Irrational numbers cannot be written in the p/q form.

There is a unique real number which can be represented on a number line.

If r is one such rational number and s is an irrational number, then (r + s), (r − s), (r × s) and (r/s) are irrational.

For positive real numbers, the corresponding identities hold together:

ab−−√ab = a−−√×b√a×b

ab−−√ab = a√b√ab

(a−−√+b√)×(a−−√−b√)=a−b(a+b)×(a−b)=a−b

(a+b√)×(a−b√)=a2−b(a+b)×(a−b)=a2−b

(a−−√+b√)2=a2+2ab−−√+b(a+b)2=a2+2ab+b

If you want to rationalize the denominator of 1/√ (a + b), then we have to multiply it by √(a − b)/√(a − b), where a and b are both the integers.

Suppose a is a real number (greater than 0) and p and q are the rational numbers.

ap x bq = (ab)p+q

(ap)q = apq

ap / aq = (a)p-q

ap / bp = (ab)p

Class 9 Maths Formulas For Polynomials

A polynomial p(x) denoted for one variable 'x' comprises an algebraic expression in the form:

p(x) = anxn + an-1xn-1 + ... + a2x2 + a1x + a0 ; where a0, a1, a2, ... an are constants where an ≠ 0

Any real number; let's say 'a' is considered to be the zero of a polynomial 'p(x)' if p(a) = 0. In this case, a is said to be the root of the equation p(x) = 0.

Every one variable linear polynomial will contain a unique zero, a real number which is a zero of the zero polynomial and non-zero constant polynomial which does not have any zeros.

Remainder Theorem: If p(x) has the degree greater than or equal to 1 and p(x) when divided by the linear polynomial x – a will give the remainder as p(a).

Factor Theorem: x – a will be the factor of the polynomial p(x), whenever p(a) = 0. The vice-versa also holds true every time.

Class 9 Maths Formulas For Coordinate Geometry

Whenever you have to locate an object on a plane, you need two divide the plane into two perpendicular lines, thereby, making it a Cartesian Plane.

The horizontal line is known as the x-axis and the vertical line is called the y-axis.

The coordinates of a point are in the form of (+, +) in the first quadrant, (–, +) in the second quadrant, (–, –) in the third quadrant and (+, –) in the fourth quadrant; where + and – denotes the positive and the negative real number respectively.

The coordinates of the origin are (0, 0) and thereby it gets up to move in the positive and negative number.

9th Class Formulas For Algebraic Identities

Given below are the algebraic identities which are considered very important maths formulas for Class 9.

(a + b)2 = a2 + 2ab + b2

(a – b)2 = a2 – 2ab + b2

(a + b) (a – b) = a2 -b2

(x + a) (x + b) = x2 + (a + b) x + ab

$(x + a) (x - b) = x2 + (a - b) x - ab$

$(x - a) (x + b) = x2 + (b - a) x - ab$

$(x - a) (x - b) = x2 - (a + b) x + ab$

$(a + b)3 = a3 + b3 + 3ab (a + b)$

$(a - b)3 = a3 - b3 - 3ab (a - b)$

$(x + y + z)2 = x2 + y2 + z2 + 2xy + 2yz + 2xz$

$(x + y - z)2 = x2 + y2 + z2 + 2xy - 2yz - 2xz$

$(x - y + z)2 = x2 + y2 + z2 - 2xy - 2yz + 2xz$

$(x - y - z)2 = x2 + y2 + z2 - 2xy + 2yz - 2xz$

$x3 + y3 + z3 - 3xyz = (x + y + z) (x2 + y2 + z2 - xy - yz -xz)$

$x2 + y2 = 1212 [(x + y)2 + (x - y)2]$

$(x + a) (x + b) (x + c) = x3 + (a + b + c)x2 + (ab + bc + ca)x + abc$

$x3 + y3 = (x + y) (x2 - xy + y2)$

$x3 - y3 = (x - y) (x2 + xy + y2)$

$x2 + y2 + z2 - xy - yz - zx = 1212 [(x - y)2 + (y - z)2 + (z - x)2]$

Class 9 Maths Formulas For Triangles

A triangle is a closed geometrical figure formed by three sides and three angles.

Two figures are congruent if they have the same shape and same size.

If the two triangles ABC and DEF are congruent under the correspondence that A ↔ D, B ↔ E and C ↔ F, then symbolically, these can be expressed as Δ ABC ≅ Δ DEF.

Right Angled Triangle: Pythagoras Theorem

Suppose Δ ABC is a right-angled triangle with AB as the perpendicular, BC as the base and AC as the hypotenuse; then Pythagoras Theorem will be expressed as:

$(Hypotenuse)2 = (Perpendicular)2 + (Base)2$

i.e. $(AC)2 = (AB)2 + (BC)2$

Class 9 Maths Formulas For Areas Of Parallelograms And Triangles

A parallelogram is a type of quadrilateral which contains parallel opposite sides.

Area of parallelogram = Base × Height

Area of Triangle = 1212 × Base × Height

Class 9 Maths Formulas For Circle

A circle is a closed geometrical figure. All points on the boundary of a circle are equidistance from a fixed point inside the circle (called the centre).

Area of a circle (of radius r) = π × r2

The diameter of the circle, d = 2 × r

Circumference of the circle = 2 × π × r

Sector angle of the circle, θ = (180 × l) / (π × r)

Area of the sector = (θ/2) × r2; where θ is the angle between the two radii

Area of the circular ring = π × (R2 – r2); where R – radius of the outer circle and r – radius of the inner circle

Class 9 Maths Heron's Formula

Heron's Formula is used to calculate the area of a triangle whose all three sides are known. Let's suppose the length of three sides are a, b and c.

Step 1 – Calculate the semi-perimeter, s=a+b+c2s=a+b+c2

Step 2 – Area of the triangle = s(s–a)(s–b)(s–c)------------------√s(s–a)(s–b)(s–c)

Class 9 Maths Formulas For Surface Areas And Volumes

Here, LSA stands for Lateral/Curved Surface Area and TSA stands for Total Surface Area.

Name of the Solid FigureFormulas

CuboidLSA: 2h(l + b)
TSA: 2(lb + bh + hl)
Volume: l × b × h

l = length,
b = breadth,
h = height
CubeLSA: 4a2
TSA: 6a2
Volume: a3

a = sides of a cube
Right Circular CylinderLSA: 2(π × r × h)
TSA: 2πr (r + h)
Volume: π × r2 × h

r = radius,
h = height
Right PyramidLSA: ½ × p × l
TSA: LSA + Area of the base
Volume: ⅓ × Area of the base × h

p = perimeter of the base,
l = slant height, h = height
PrismLSA: p × h
TSA: LSA × 2B
Volume: B × h

p = perimeter of the base,
B = area of base, h = height
Right Circular ConeLSA: πrl
TSA: π × r × (r + l)

Volume: ⅓ × (πr2h)

r = radius,
l = slant height,
h = height
    HemisphereLSA: 2 × π × r2
TSA: 3 × π × r2
Volume: ⅔ × (πr3)

r = radius
    SphereLSA: 4 × π × r2
TSA: 4 × π × r2
Volume: 4/3 × (πr3)

r = radius
    Class 9 Maths Formulas For Statistics
    Certain facts or figures which can be collected or transformed into some useful purpose are known as data. These data can be graphically represented to increase readability for people.
    Three measures of formulas to interpret the ungrouped data:
    CategoryMathematical Formulas
    Mean, x‾x‾∑xn∑xn
x = Sum of the values; N = Number of values
    Standard   Deviation, σσσ=∑ni=1(xi−x‾‾‾)2N−1−−−−−−−−−√σ=∑i=1n(xi−x‾)2N−1

xi = Terms Given in the Data, x‾ = Mean, N = Total number of Terms
    Range, RR = Largest data value − Smallest data value

Variance, σ^2 $=\frac{\sum x_i - \bar{x}}{N}$

x = Item given in the data, $\bar{x}$ = Mean of the data,
n = Total number of items

Class 9 Maths Formulas For Probability

Probability is the possibility of any event likely to happen. The probability of any event can only be from 0 to 1 with 0 being no chances and 1 being the possibility of that event to happen.

Probability=Number of favourable outcomes / Total Number of outcomes